All about my **AMAZING** Dad!

My Dad is _____ years old. His favorite food is _____

_____

and he loves to watch _____

_____

I think my Dad looks the most handsome

when _____

Three words I would use to describe my Dad.

I'm thankful for
my Dad because

My **SUPERSTAR** Dad!

My Dad is _____ at so many things.

But he is the best 🏆 at _____

_____

I admire my Dad because

My INCREDIBLE Dad!

My Dad is my _____

When I grow up, I want to be as_____

and _____

as my Dad!

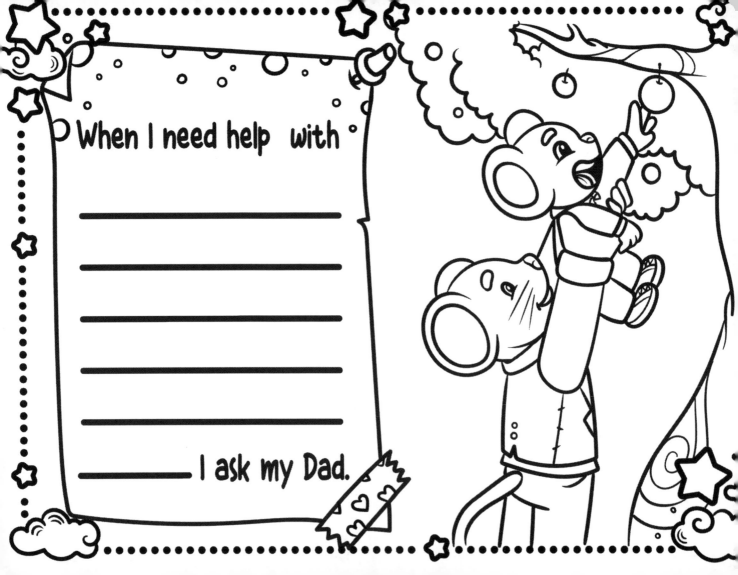

When I need help with

_____

_____

_____

_____

_____ I ask my Dad.

My favorite thing
about Dad is

_____

_____

_____

_____

Draw your Dad's favorite
thing in the box!

My Dad makes me laugh when

My AWESOME Dad!

My Dad is the _____ Dad. He is funny

when he _____. He always

makes me _____. I love it when

Dad _____

My Dad taught me how to

My **SUPERHERO** Dad!

My Dad's superhero name is

_____

_____

His superpower is _____

_____

_____

MY **SUPERDAD!**

My Dad knows how to

_____

_____

_____

_____

better than anyone.

I L♥VE my Dad!

My dad is cooler than _____

stronger than _____

and more handsome than _____

Grrrrr!

_____

My Dad is proud
of me when I

_____

_____

_____

_____

_____

DADDY and ME !

My Dad and I

_____

_____

_____

_____

when we spend time together.

a drawing of me and dad

My Dad is always
there for me when

_____

_____

_____

_____

I'm so happy when my Dad

When my Dad is driving, he

_____

_____

_____

_____

I inherited _____

_____

_____

_____

_____

from my Dad.

When I get older. I hope
my Dad and I can

_____

_____

_____

_____

My favorite memory
of my Dad

_____

_____

_____

_____

_____

Date: ....

My favorite memory of
Me and Dad!

I'm my Daddy's biggest fan because

- ☐ He's strong
- ☐ He makes me laugh all the times
- ☐ He's very kind
- ☐ He gives the best hugs
- ☐ He's the most handsome Dad
- ☐ He has superpowers
- ☐ _____
- ☐ _____

My Favorite Picture of Dad!

Date: _____

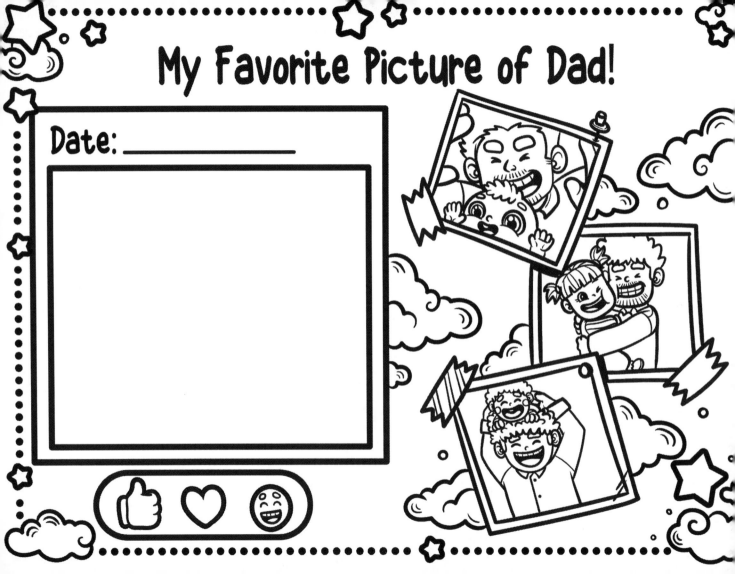

My Dad is the happiest

when _____

_____

_____

_____

My Dad's perfect
day would be

On this special day, I want
my Dad to know

_____

_____

_____

_____

Special Coupons for Daddy!
(Color the star when claimed)

ONE BIG HUG

A GOOD BACK MASSAGE

Daddy, I wrote a poem for you

Thank you for being an Awesome Dad !

Made in the USA
Coppell, TX
15 June 2022

78850408R00020